The Updates of Google Algorithm

Understanding how AI and search changes are reshaping the internet and its consequences for web traffic.

Brent T. Lowe

Copyright©2024 [Brent T. Lowe]

All rights reserved. No part of this publication may be reproduced, distributed, or transmitted in any form or by any means, including photocopying, recording, or other electronic or mechanical methods, without the prior written permission of the publisher, except in the case of brief quotations embodied in critical reviews and certain other noncommercial uses permitted by copyright law.

TABLE OF CONTENT

Introduction **4**

Chapter 1 .... **8**
   The Evolution of Google Search 8

Chapter 2 .... **18**
   Understanding SEO: Past and Present 18

Chapter 3 .... **26**
   The September 2023 Update: A Turning Point 26

Chapter 3 .... **36**
   The March 2024 Update: Further Disruptions 36

Chapter 4 .... **44**
   AI Overviews: Google's New Frontier 44

Chapter 6 .... **60**
   The Rise of User-Generated Content 60

Chapter 7 .... **70**
   Case Study: House Fresh's Struggle 70

Chapter 8 .... **76**
   Adapting to Change: Strategies for Survival 76

Chapter 9 .... **82**
   The Role of Content Quality 82

Chapter 10 .... **88**
   Google's War on Spam 88

Chapter 11 ....**94**
AI and Search Accuracy 94
Chapter 12 ....**100**
The Business Side: Financial Implications............100
Chapter 13 ....**106**
Legal and Ethical Considerations 106
Chapter 14 ....**112**
The Future of Search 112
Conclusion **118**

Introduction

In the ever-evolving landscape of the internet, Google's search engine reigns supreme. It's the gateway through which billions of user's access information, services, and entertainment. From its humble beginnings as a university project in the late 1990s, Google has grown into a behemoth that dominates over 90% of the global search market. The key to its success lies in its powerful and sophisticated search algorithm, which has undergone numerous transformations to improve the quality of search results and user experience.

However, in recent years, Google has embarked on a series of dramatic updates to its algorithm, fundamentally altering how it evaluates and ranks web content. These changes have been driven by the incorporation of artificial intelligence (AI) and machine learning technologies, aimed at making search results more relevant and useful. While these updates promise a more intuitive and helpful search experience, they have also sparked significant controversy and upheaval among website owners, content creators, and digital marketers.

This book explores the profound impact of Google's recent algorithm updates, focusing on two pivotal changes: The September 2023 update and the March 2024 update. These updates, part of Google's ongoing effort to prioritize high-quality, user-focused content, have had far-reaching consequences for the internet ecosystem. Small, independent websites, which once thrived by providing niche, expert content, have found themselves struggling to maintain visibility and traffic. Conversely, platforms featuring user-generated content, like Reddit and Quora, have seen an unprecedented surge in search traffic.

At the heart of these changes is Google's new AI feature known as "AI Overviews." Introduced to provide concise, AI-generated answers to user queries, this tool represents a significant shift from Google's traditional search model. Instead of directing users to external websites, AI Overviews aim to deliver information directly within the search results page. While this innovation has the potential to enhance user convenience, it also raises critical questions about content ownership, accuracy, and the future of web traffic.

The story of House Fresh, a website dedicated to air purifier reviews, exemplifies the challenges faced by many niche content creators. Founded on rigorous, science-based testing, HouseFresh initially flourished under Google's algorithms, only to see its traffic decimated by the recent updates. This case, along with many others, illustrates the precarious balance between creating quality content and navigating the capricious nature of search engine algorithms.

In this book, we delve into the mechanics of Google's search algorithm, dissect the specific updates, and analyze their impact on various types of websites. We explore the broader implications for the digital landscape, including the rise of user-generated content platforms, the shifting strategies of SEO, and the ethical and legal challenges posed by Google's immense power over web traffic.

Moreover, we examine how content creators and website owners can adapt to these changes. From understanding what Google now prioritizes in its search results to exploring alternative traffic sources and diversifying content strategies, this book provides practical insights and advice for navigating the new search environment.

The recent updates mark a turning point in the evolution of search technology, one that blends AI's capabilities with traditional search principles. As Google continues to refine and expand its algorithm, the internet as we know it is being reshaped. This book aims to shed light on these transformations, offering a comprehensive guide to understanding and adapting to the new realities of search.

By exploring the intersection of technology, business, and content creation, we aim to provide a thorough analysis of Google's algorithm updates and their implications for the future. Whether you are a website owner, a digital marketer, or simply an interested observer of technological trends, this book will equip you with the knowledge and tools to navigate the rapidly changing digital landscape.

Chapter 1

The Evolution of Google Search

The Rise of the Search Engine Giant

Google's ascent to dominance in the search engine market is a tale of innovation, strategic vision, and relentless pursuit of excellence. Founded in 1998 by Larry Page and Sergey Brin, two Ph.D. students at Stanford University, Google started as a research project aimed at improving the way information was retrieved on the burgeoning World Wide Web. At the time, existing search engines like AltaVista and Yahoo! primarily ranked search results based on the frequency of keywords on web pages, often leading to irrelevant or low-quality results.

Page and Brin introduced a revolutionary approach called PageRank, an algorithm that analyzed the links between web pages to determine their importance and relevance. By treating links as votes of confidence from one page to another, PageRank provided a more nuanced and effective way to rank search results. This innovation quickly set Google apart from its competitors, offering users more accurate and reliable information.

Google's minimalist homepage, characterized by its clean design and prominent search bar, also contributed to its popularity. Unlike other search engines cluttered with advertisements and portal features, Google's focus on simplicity and speed resonated with users. The company's mission, "to organize the world's information and make it universally accessible and useful," guided its development and expansion.

In the early 2000s, Google solidified its position as the leading search engine. Strategic acquisitions, such as the purchase of Applied Semantics in 2003 (which led to the creation of Google AdSense), and the introduction of innovative products like Google News and Google Maps, further enhanced its ecosystem. By continuously improving its core search technology and expanding its range of services, Google ensured its growth and influence.

Early Algorithm Updates and Their Impact

As the web grew exponentially, so did the challenges of maintaining high-quality search results. In response, Google began refining its search algorithm through a series of updates designed to combat spam, improve relevance, and enhance the user experience. These early algorithm updates laid the foundation for the sophisticated search engine we know today.

1. **Florida Update (2003)**

One of the first major updates, the Florida Update, targeted websites that engaged in manipulative SEO practices, such as keyword stuffing and hidden text. These tactics were commonly used to artificially inflate a site's rankings, often at the expense of user experience. The Florida Update aimed to level the playing field by penalizing such practices and rewarding sites with genuinely valuable content. While it caused significant upheaval for many websites reliant on black-hat SEO techniques, it ultimately improved the quality of search results.

2. **Jagger Update (2005)**

The Jagger Update continued Google's crackdown on low-quality and manipulative SEO practices. It focused on eliminating link farms and paid links, which were schemes where websites exchanged or purchased links to boost their rankings artificially. Jagger reinforced the importance of natural, earned backlinks, ensuring that link equity was awarded based on merit rather than manipulation. This update also emphasized the need for high-quality, relevant content, further aligning search results with user intent.

3. Big Daddy Update (2005-2006)

The Big Daddy Update introduced significant changes to Google's infrastructure, improving the way it handled and indexed web pages. It addressed issues related to canonicalization (the process of determining the preferred version of a URL when multiple versions exist), redirect handling, and duplicate content. Big Daddy aimed to provide more accurate and comprehensive search results by ensuring that Google's index reflected the most relevant and authoritative pages.

4. Vince Update (2009)

The Vince Update marked a shift in Google's approach to ranking, favoring established brands and authoritative websites. While not as comprehensive as other updates, Vince recognized that well-known brands often provided more reliable and trustworthy information. This update aimed to enhance user trust in search results by prioritizing reputable sources, a move that benefited large, established websites and businesses.

5. Caffeine Update (2010)

The Caffeine Update was a significant overhaul of Google's indexing system, designed to provide fresher and more up-to-date search results. By improving the speed and efficiency of its indexing process, Google ensured that new content was quickly available to users. This update also laid the groundwork for integrating real-time data from sources like social media, enhancing the search engine's ability to deliver timely and relevant information.

6. Panda Update (2011)

The Panda Update represented a major shift in Google's fight against low-quality content. Named after one of its lead engineers, Navneet Panda, the update targeted "content farms" and sites with thin or duplicated content. Panda introduced a site-wide penalty, meaning that if a significant portion of a website was deemed low quality, the entire site could suffer in rankings. This update emphasized the importance of original, high-quality content and user engagement metrics, such as time spent on site and bounce rate.

7. Penguin Update (2012)

The Penguin Update focused on combating web spam, particularly practices related to unnatural link profiles and over-optimization. It penalized sites that engaged in manipulative link-building strategies, such as acquiring links from low-quality or irrelevant sources. Penguin aimed to reward sites with natural, earned backlinks and discourage attempts to game the system. This update reinforced the importance of ethical SEO practices and the value of high-quality, relevant content.

8. Hummingbird Update (2013)

The Hummingbird Update was a significant reengineering of Google's core algorithm, designed to better understand the meaning behind search queries. Unlike previous updates that targeted specific issues, Hummingbird improved the algorithm's ability to interpret complex, conversational queries and provide more accurate results. It introduced the concept of semantic search, which considered the context and intent behind a user's query rather than relying solely on keywords. This update laid the foundation for future advancements in natural language processing and AI integration.

9. Mobilegeddon (2015)

Recognizing the growing importance of mobile internet usage, Google introduced the Mobilegeddon Update to prioritize mobile-friendly websites in search results. This update rewarded sites that provided a positive user experience on mobile devices and penalized those that did not. Mobilegeddon underscored the importance of responsive design and mobile optimization, ensuring that users could access high-quality content regardless of the device they used.

10. Rank Brain (2015)

RankBrain marked the introduction of machine learning into Google's search algorithm. As part of the Hummingbird algorithm, RankBrain helped Google better interpret and process complex search queries. It used artificial intelligence to identify patterns and improve the relevance of search results, particularly for queries that Google had not encountered before. RankBrain represented a significant leap forward in search technology, enhancing the algorithm's ability to deliver more accurate and relevant results.

From its inception, Google has been at the forefront of search technology, continuously refining and evolving its algorithm to provide the best possible user experience. The early algorithm updates played a crucial role in shaping the quality and relevance of search results, setting the stage for the sophisticated, AI-driven search engine we rely on today. As Google continues to innovate and integrate advanced technologies like AI and machine learning, its impact on the internet landscape will only grow. Understanding the history and evolution of Google's search algorithm provides valuable insights into the future of search and the ongoing challenges and opportunities for website owners and digital marketers.

Chapter 2

Understanding SEO: Past and Present

The Basics of SEO

Search Engine Optimization (SEO) is a multifaceted strategy aimed at improving a website's visibility in search engine results pages (SERPs). The goal is to attract organic traffic, which is crucial for the success of any online presence, whether it's a blog, an e-commerce site, or a corporate website. At its core, SEO revolves around understanding how search engines like Google rank and display content, and then optimizing a site to align with these criteria.

SEO is broadly divided into two main categories: on-page SEO and off-page SEO.

On-page SEO refers to the optimization strategies implemented directly on the website. This includes:

1. **Keyword Research and Optimization:** Identifying relevant keywords that potential visitors are likely to use in search queries and

incorporating these keywords strategically into content, headings, meta descriptions, and tags.
2. **Content Quality:** Creating high-quality, valuable, and engaging content that meets the needs and interests of the target audience. Search engines prioritize content that provides a good user experience, is comprehensive, and includes relevant keywords naturally.
3. **Technical SEO:** Ensuring the website is technically sound. This involves improving site speed, ensuring mobile-friendliness, using clean and efficient code, creating an XML sitemap, and enabling a secure HTTPS protocol.
4. **User Experience (UX):** Enhancing the overall user experience by improving site navigation, layout, and design. A positive UX keeps visitors on the site longer, reduces bounce rates, and increases the likelihood of conversions.
5. **Internal Linking:** Creating a robust internal linking structure that helps search engines understand the hierarchy and importance of pages, while also improving user navigation.

Off-page SEO involves actions taken outside the website to impact its rankings within SERPs. This primarily focuses on:

1. **Backlinks:** Acquiring high-quality backlinks from authoritative and relevant websites. Backlinks act as votes of confidence and can significantly influence a site's ranking.
2. **Social Signals:** Leveraging social media platforms to drive traffic and engagement, indirectly contributing to a site's search visibility.
3. **Brand Mentions:** Encouraging mentions of the brand across the web, which can enhance credibility and authority.
4. **Guest Blogging:** Writing articles for other websites within the same industry to gain exposure and valuable backlinks.

SEO is dynamic and continually evolving. It requires ongoing efforts to stay abreast of algorithm changes, industry trends, and shifts in user behavior.

SEO Tactics Then and Now
SEO Tactics Then: The Early Days

In the early days of the internet, SEO was relatively straightforward but often exploitative. Here are some of the tactics that were prevalent:

1. **Keyword Stuffing:** Early SEO heavily relied on the frequency of keywords. Webmasters would cram as many keywords as possible into their content, often at the expense of readability and user experience. For instance, an article about "best running shoes" might have the phrase "best running shoes" repeated excessively to signal relevance to search engines.
2. **Meta Tag Manipulation:** Meta tags, including the meta description and meta keywords, were heavily used to signal the content of a webpage to search engines. SEO practitioners would stuff these tags with keywords, regardless of the actual content.
3. **Hidden Text and Links**: Some webmasters would hide keywords and links within their web pages by matching the text color to the background color, making them invisible to users but readable by search engines. This tactic was used to manipulate rankings without impacting the visible content.

4. **Link Farms:** To increase the number of backlinks, which were a significant ranking factor, SEO practitioners created networks of websites that existed solely to link to each other. These link farms inflated the perceived authority and relevance of a site artificially.
5. **Doorway Pages:** These were low-quality pages created to rank for specific keywords and then redirect visitors to a different, often unrelated, page. The primary goal was to capture search engine traffic through deceptive means.
6. **Exact Match Domains (EMDs):** Early SEO placed a lot of emphasis on domain names. Websites with exact match domains, such as "best-running-shoes.com," often ranked higher purely based on their domain name, regardless of content quality.

SEO Tactics Now: Modern Best Practices

Modern SEO is far more sophisticated and user-focused. Search engines like Google have become adept at identifying and penalizing manipulative tactics, leading to a more holistic approach to SEO that emphasizes quality, relevance, and user satisfaction.

1. **Quality Content Creation:** Content is king in modern SEO. High-quality, informative, and engaging content that meets the needs of the audience is paramount. This content should be well-researched, original, and comprehensive, providing real value to users.
2. **Semantic Search and LSI Keywords:** Instead of focusing solely on exact match keywords, modern SEO uses Latent Semantic Indexing (LSI) keywords, which are terms related to the main keyword. This approach aligns with the way search engines understand context and meaning, rather than just matching keywords.
3. **Mobile Optimization:** With the increasing use of mobile devices for internet access, mobile optimization is critical. Websites must be responsive and provide a seamless user experience across different devices. Google's mobile-first indexing further underscores the importance of mobile-friendly sites.
4. **User Experience (UX):** Modern SEO places a significant emphasis on UX. Factors such as site speed, easy navigation, clean design, and low bounce rates contribute to a better user experience, which in turn can positively impact rankings.

5. **Voice Search Optimization**: With the rise of smart speakers and voice assistants, optimizing for voice search is becoming increasingly important. This involves using more natural language in content and focusing on long-tail keywords that match conversational queries.
6. **Structured Data and Schema Markup:** Structured data helps search engines understand the content of a page more clearly. Implementing schema markup can enhance search visibility and provide rich snippets in search results, leading to higher click-through rates.
7. **Secure Websites (HTTPS)**: Security is a priority for modern users and search engines alike. Using HTTPS instead of HTTP is a ranking factor and assures users that their data is protected.
8. **Local SEO:** For businesses with a physical presence, local SEO is crucial. This involves optimizing for location-based searches, managing local listings, and encouraging reviews on platforms like Google My Business.
9. **Content Marketing and Social Media Integration:** Creating shareable content and leveraging social media platforms to drive engagement and traffic is a key aspect of

modern SEO. Social signals, while not direct ranking factors, can influence search visibility and brand awareness.
11. **Continuous Adaptation and Learning:** Modern SEO is an ongoing process. Keeping up with algorithm updates, industry trends, and changes in user behavior is essential. SEO practitioners must be agile, constantly adapting their strategies to stay ahead in the competitive digital landscape.

The evolution of SEO from its early days of keyword stuffing and link farms to the sophisticated, user-centric strategies of today reflects the broader changes in how search engines operate and prioritize content. Understanding both the history and current best practices of SEO is crucial for anyone looking to succeed in the digital world. By focusing on quality, relevance, and user experience, modern SEO not only enhances search visibility but also builds a sustainable and reputable online presence.

Chapter 3

The September 2023 Update: A Turning Point

Overview of the Changes

The September 2023 update to Google's search algorithm marked a significant turning point in the way search results are generated and displayed. This update was part of a broader series of changes aimed at enhancing user experience, combating spam, and prioritizing high-quality content. The overhaul, while intended to refine search results, had widespread repercussions for many website owners, particularly those relying heavily on organic search traffic.

The primary focus of the September 2023 update was to further emphasize the principles outlined in Google's Helpful Content Update of 2022. The key changes included:

1. **Enhanced Content Quality Filters:** Google refined its ability to distinguish between high-quality and low-quality content. The algorithm

became better at identifying original, well-researched articles and differentiating them from content that was merely optimized for search engines without adding real value to readers.

2. **User Intent Alignment:** The update improved the search engine's understanding of user intent. This meant that search results were more accurately tailored to what users were genuinely seeking, rather than just matching keywords. Google's algorithm began to weigh context and user behavior more heavily, ensuring that the content served was more relevant and useful.

3. **Reduction of Redundant and Duplicate Content:** Websites that relied on republishing or slightly modifying existing content found themselves losing visibility. The update was particularly harsh on sites that engaged in content scraping or offered little to no unique value beyond what was already available on the web.

4. **Increased Importance of E-A-T**: Expertise, Authoritativeness, and Trustworthiness (E-A-T) became even more critical. Google enhanced its evaluation criteria to ensure that content from reputable sources, written by experts, and

backed by reliable information ranked higher. This shift disadvantaged sites with vague author credentials or dubious content.

5. **AI-Generated Content Scrutiny: As** AI-generated content proliferated, Google implemented more robust mechanisms to detect and demote content produced by AI tools unless it was clearly marked and met high-quality standards. This change aimed to curb the flood of generic, machine-generated articles that lacked depth and originality.

6. **Visual and Multimedia Content:** The update placed greater emphasis on multimedia content. Websites that effectively utilized images, videos, and interactive elements saw a boost in rankings. This move was designed to enhance user engagement and satisfaction by offering diverse content formats.

7. **User Experience and Core Web Vitals:** Google continued to prioritize user experience metrics, particularly Core Web Vitals, which include loading speed, interactivity, and visual stability. Websites that failed to meet these benchmarks saw significant drops in their search rankings.

Immediate Impacts on Websites

The immediate aftermath of the September 2023 update was tumultuous for many website owners and digital marketers. The changes brought about a dramatic reshuffling of search rankings, with significant winners and losers emerging overnight.

1. **Impact on Small and Independent Websites:** One of the most striking outcomes was the adverse effect on small and independent websites. Many site owners who had previously adhered to SEO best practices found their traffic plummeting. Websites that relied on niche topics, despite offering high-quality and original content, struggled to maintain their visibility.

   The algorithm's preference for established brands and authoritative sources made it challenging for smaller players to compete. For instance, Gisele Navarro's website, HouseFresh, which focused on air purifier reviews, experienced a devastating decline in traffic. Despite offering scientifically rigorous and well-researched content, HouseFresh saw its visibility diminish as search results began favoring larger lifestyle publications with less specialized knowledge.

2. Rise of User-Generated Content Platforms: Platforms like Reddit, Quora, and Instagram saw a substantial increase in traffic from Google search. This shift was partly due to the growing trend of users seeking peer reviews and personal experiences. User-generated content was perceived as more authentic and trustworthy, aligning with Google's aim to surface helpful and relevant content. Reddit, in particular, experienced a 126% growth in search traffic, reflecting a broader shift towards community-driven information sources.

3. **Decline of Traditional Media Sites:** Even established media outlets were not immune to the upheaval. Websites like New York Magazine and GQ reported significant drops in their search traffic. This decline was attributed to the algorithm's refined focus on content quality and user intent, which sometimes worked against traditional media sites that relied on broad, less targeted content.

4. **Challenges for E-Commerce and Affiliate Sites:** E-commerce and affiliate marketing

sites, which often depended on SEO to drive sales, faced a tough battle. Many of these sites relied on product reviews and comparison articles that were hit hard by the update. Google's enhanced content quality filters made it difficult for these sites to rank unless they provided exceptional value and original insights.

5. **Technical SEO Adjustments:** Websites with technical SEO issues, such as slow loading times, poor mobile optimization, and intrusive ads, saw their rankings suffer. The emphasis on Core Web Vitals and overall user experience meant that technical deficiencies could no longer be overlooked. Site owners had to prioritize improving their site's performance and user experience to recover lost traffic.

6. **Content Creators and Bloggers**: Individual content creators and bloggers, particularly those without a strong brand presence, struggled to maintain their visibility. The update's focus on E-A-T meant that content from well-known experts and authorities was favored over personal blogs. This shift required content creators to bolster their credentials and ensure their content met the highest standards of accuracy and trustworthiness.

Case Studies
Case Study 1: Ready Steady Cut

Ready Steady Cut, a UK-based entertainment news site, experienced an immediate and severe drop in traffic following the September 2023 update. Editor-in-chief Daniel Hart reported that their traffic halved overnight and continued to decline. Despite their efforts to follow Google's guidelines and improve their content, they couldn't regain their previous visibility. The site was forced to downsize significantly, reducing its team of 20 writers and editors to just four. This case exemplifies the challenges faced by niche sites that were unable to compete with larger, more established brands in the wake of the update.

Case Study 2: HouseFresh

HouseFresh, mentioned earlier, also faced drastic consequences. The website, which provided detailed air purifier reviews based on scientific testing, saw its traffic dwindle as Google began favoring larger lifestyle publications. This shift highlighted a perceived disconnect between Google's stated aim of promoting high-quality content and the actual results of the algorithm update. Despite following SEO best practices and producing valuable content, HouseFresh struggled to compete against the authority and reach of bigger websites.

Case Study 3: Reddit

In stark contrast, Reddit emerged as a major beneficiary of the update. The platform's extensive user-generated content and active communities resonated with Google's focus on authentic, helpful information. Reddit's growth in search traffic underscored the increasing preference for content that reflects real user experiences and insights. This case demonstrates how platforms that foster community engagement and provide diverse viewpoints can thrive in the evolving search landscape.

The September 2023 update was a watershed moment in the evolution of Google's search algorithm. While it aimed to enhance the quality and relevance of search results, the immediate impacts were profoundly disruptive for many website owners. Small and independent sites, in particular, found themselves at a disadvantage as the algorithm favored established brands and authoritative sources. The rise of user-generated content platforms like Reddit indicated a shift towards valuing personal experiences and community-driven insights.

For digital marketers, content creators, and website owners, the update underscored the importance of adapting to an ever-changing search landscape. Success in the post-update era requires a commitment to producing high-quality, original content, enhancing user experience, and continually refining SEO strategies to align with evolving algorithms. As Google continues to refine its approach, the lessons learned from the September 2023 update will remain critical for navigating the future of search.

Chapter 3

The March 2024 Update: Further Disruptions

Details of the Update

The March 2024 update to Google's search algorithm built upon the controversial September 2023 update, introducing further refinements and adjustments aimed at enhancing search quality and user experience. While Google framed these changes as necessary for improving the relevance and reliability of search results, the update triggered significant disruptions across the web, impacting a wide range of websites and online businesses.

The March 2024 update included several key components:

1. **Advanced AI Integration:** Google further integrated its AI capabilities into the search algorithm, enhancing its ability to understand and interpret complex queries. This integration allowed for more nuanced responses and better

alignment with user intent. The AI enhancements were designed to provide more accurate and contextually relevant results, but they also increased the complexity of the algorithm.
2. **Stringent Content Authenticity Checks:** The update introduced more rigorous checks for content authenticity and credibility. Websites needed to demonstrate clear expertise and authoritativeness to rank well. This change particularly affected sites that previously relied on general information or lacked clear credentials for their authors.
3. **Focus on Multimedia Content:** Building on the emphasis from the previous update, Google placed even greater importance on multimedia content. Websites that effectively utilized videos, images, and interactive elements were rewarded with higher rankings. This shift aimed to cater to diverse user preferences and enhance overall engagement.
4. **Improved Spam Detection:** The algorithm's ability to detect and penalize spammy content was significantly enhanced. Websites employing black-hat SEO techniques, such as keyword stuffing, cloaking, or link schemes, faced severe penalties. This change aimed to clean up search

results and ensure users encountered high-quality, legitimate content.
5. **Enhanced User Experience Metrics:** Core Web Vitals and other user experience metrics continued to play a crucial role. Google refined its evaluation criteria, making it harder for websites with poor loading speeds, intrusive ads, or mobile usability issues to rank well. This change reinforced the need for websites to prioritize user-friendly designs and performance optimization.
6. **Localized Search Enhancements:** The update introduced improvements in localized search results. Businesses and websites with a strong local presence and relevant local content were more likely to appear in search results for geographically specific queries. This change aimed to provide users with more relevant local information and support local businesses.

Case Studies of Affected Websites

The March 2024 update had a profound impact on many websites, with some experiencing significant gains while others faced devastating losses. Here are a few notable case studies that illustrate the varied effects of the update:

Case Study 1: HouseFresh

HouseFresh, a website specializing in air purifier reviews, continued to struggle in the wake of the March 2024 update. Despite efforts to improve content quality and adhere to Google's guidelines, the site saw further declines in traffic. The advanced AI integration and stringent content authenticity checks made it challenging for HouseFresh to compete with larger lifestyle publications. The site, known for its detailed and scientifically rigorous reviews, found it difficult to regain its previous visibility. This case underscores the challenges faced by niche websites trying to compete against broader, more authoritative sources.

Case Study 2: Urban Dictionary

Urban Dictionary, a popular crowdsourced dictionary of slang and contemporary language, experienced a dramatic decline in search traffic. The site's reliance on user-generated content and its informal nature made it vulnerable to the new authenticity and credibility checks. Google's algorithm struggled to reconcile the value of Urban Dictionary's unique content with its stricter quality standards. As a result, the site lost a significant portion of its visibility, highlighting the difficulties faced by platforms that prioritize user contributions over traditional authoritative sources.

Case Study 3: Travel Websites

Several travel websites, including World Travel Guy, faced substantial challenges following the March 2024 update. David Leiter, the site's owner, reported that the AI-generated responses provided by Google's updated algorithm often contained inaccurate information. For instance, searches for specific travel recommendations frequently surfaced AI-generated content that misrepresented key details. This issue not only impacted traffic but also damaged the credibility of affected websites. Despite efforts to enhance content quality and provide accurate information, these sites struggled to compete with AI-generated answers, which often lacked the depth and precision required for specialized travel advice.

Case Study 4: Reddit

In contrast to the struggles faced by many websites, Reddit continued to thrive under the new algorithm. The platform's user-generated content and active communities aligned well with Google's focus on authentic, diverse perspectives. Reddit saw further increases in search traffic, reinforcing the trend observed in previous updates. The platform's ability to provide genuine user experiences and discussions made it a preferred source for many queries, especially those seeking personal insights and recommendations. Reddit's success illustrates the growing importance of community-driven content in the evolving search landscape.

Case Study 5: Small Business Websites

Many small business websites faced mixed results following the March 2024 update. Local businesses with strong online presences and relevant local content saw improvements in their search rankings, benefiting from the localized search enhancements. However, those that failed to meet the updated user experience metrics or struggled with content authenticity checks experienced declines. The update highlighted the need for small businesses to invest in high-quality content, performance optimization, and clear local relevance to maintain and improve their search visibility.

The March 2024 update to Google's search algorithm introduced significant changes that aimed to enhance the quality and relevance of search results. While the update succeeded in many respects, it also brought about widespread disruptions for numerous websites.

Advanced AI integration, stringent content authenticity checks, and a continued focus on user experience metrics created new challenges and opportunities for webmasters.

The case studies presented here illustrate the varied impacts of the update, from the continued struggles of niche sites like HouseFresh to the ongoing success of user-generated content platforms like Reddit. The experiences of travel websites, Urban Dictionary, and small businesses further highlight the complexities of navigating Google's evolving search landscape.

For website owners and digital marketers, the March 2024 update underscored the importance of adapting to changing algorithms and maintaining a commitment to high-quality, user-focused content. As Google continues to refine its approach, staying informed about algorithm updates and proactively optimizing websites will remain critical for achieving and maintaining search visibility in the competitive online environment.

Chapter 4

AI Overviews: Google's New Frontier

Introduction to AI Overviews

The digital landscape is continuously evolving, and Google remains at the forefront of these changes. One of the most transformative updates in recent years is the introduction of AI Overviews. This feature, announced by Google CEO Sundar Pichai during the company's annual developer conference in 2023, represents a significant shift in how Google processes and presents information. AI Overviews are designed to provide users with concise, AI-generated answers to their queries directly on the search results page, effectively transforming Google from a search engine into a more comprehensive search and answer engine.

The introduction of AI Overviews is part of Google's broader strategy to integrate advanced artificial intelligence into its core products, enhancing the user experience by delivering more precise and relevant information quickly. However, this new feature has sparked a considerable debate among webmasters, digital marketers, and content creators. While Google touts the benefits of AI Overviews in terms of improved efficiency and user satisfaction, critics argue that this shift could have far-reaching implications for web traffic, content creation, and the overall structure of the internet.

How AI-Generated Answers Work

AI Overviews leverage Google's advanced machine learning models, which are trained on vast amounts of data to understand and generate human-like responses. These models, such as the ones powering Google's BERT and MUM updates, are capable of interpreting complex queries, understanding context, and synthesizing information from multiple sources to provide a concise answer.

1. **Query Interpretation:** When a user enters a query into Google, the search engine first interprets the intent behind the query. This involves breaking down the query into its components and understanding the context. For example, a search for "best Italian restaurants in New York" requires understanding the user's intent to find top-rated Italian dining options in a specific location.

2. **Information Retrieval**: Once the query is interpreted, Google's AI models retrieve relevant information from its vast index of web pages. This step involves identifying and ranking content that is most likely to provide a valuable answer to the user's query. The AI prioritizes sources that are deemed authoritative and reliable, drawing from a diverse range of websites, including blogs, news sites, forums, and more.
3. **Content Synthesis:** The AI then synthesizes the retrieved information into a coherent and concise overview. This involves summarizing key points, extracting essential details, and presenting the information in a user-friendly format. For instance, an AI Overview for the query about Italian restaurants might list the top three restaurants, along with brief descriptions, ratings, and links to reviews.
4. **Presentation:** Finally, the AI-generated answer is presented at the top of the search results page. This summary is designed to be easily digestible, allowing users to quickly find the information they need without having to click through multiple links. The AI Overview typically includes a link to the sources from

which the information was drawn, enabling users to explore further if they wish.

Implications for Web Traffic and Content Creation

The introduction of AI Overviews has profound implications for web traffic and content creation. By providing direct answers to queries on the search results page, Google reduces the need for users to visit external websites, potentially diminishing the traffic that these sites receive. This shift poses significant challenges for webmasters and content creators who rely on search traffic to sustain their businesses.

1. **Reduced Click-Through Rates (CTR):** One of the immediate impacts of AI Overviews is a reduction in click-through rates for traditional search results. When users find the information they need directly on the search results page, they are less likely to click on the links below the AI Overview. This can lead to a decline in organic traffic for websites, particularly those that previously ranked highly for informational queries.

2. **Content Duplication and Attribution:** Another concern is the issue of content duplication and attribution. AI Overviews often aggregate information from multiple sources, summarizing it into a single response. This process raises questions about proper attribution and the potential for content to be used without adequate credit to the original creators. While Google includes links to source material, these links are often less prominent, reducing the visibility and recognition of the contributing websites.
3. **Impact on Small and Independent Websites:** Small and independent websites are particularly vulnerable to the changes brought about by AI Overviews. These sites often rely heavily on organic search traffic for their survival. With AI-generated answers taking precedence, many smaller sites may find it difficult to compete with larger, more established sources that are more likely to be featured in AI Overviews.
4. **Shift in Content Strategy:** The advent of AI Overviews necessitates a shift in content strategy for many websites. To remain relevant and visible in search results, content creators must focus on producing high-quality,

authoritative content that stands out as a valuable resource. This might involve investing in original research, expert insights, and multimedia content that can't be easily replicated by AI models. Additionally, optimizing content for featured snippets and rich results becomes even more critical.

5. **User Experience and Engagement:** On the positive side, AI Overviews can enhance user experience by providing quick and accurate answers to queries. This efficiency can lead to higher user satisfaction and engagement with Google as a platform. For content creators, this means that creating content that complements AI Overviews, such as in-depth articles, videos, and interactive elements, can help capture and retain user attention.

The Future of AI Overviews

As Google continues to refine its AI capabilities, the role of AI Overviews is likely to expand. Future updates may see even more sophisticated AI-generated content, with the ability to handle increasingly complex queries and provide more nuanced answers. This evolution will further blur the lines between traditional search and AI-powered responses, challenging the existing dynamics of web traffic and content creation.

1. **Enhanced Personalization:** One potential direction for AI Overviews is enhanced personalization. By leveraging user data and preferences, Google could tailor AI-generated answers to better suit individual needs and interests. This would make search results even more relevant and useful, but it also raises concerns about privacy and data security.
2. **Integration with Other Google Services:** AI Overviews could become more deeply integrated with other Google services, such as Google Assistant, Maps, and Shopping. This integration would create a more seamless and comprehensive user experience, but it could also consolidate Google's dominance in the digital ecosystem, making it even harder for other platforms and websites to compete.
3. **Ethical and Regulatory Considerations:** As AI Overviews become more prevalent, ethical and regulatory considerations will come to the forefront. Issues such as content ownership, accuracy, and bias in AI-generated responses will need to be addressed. Ensuring

transparency in how AI Overviews are generated and providing clear pathways for content creators to dispute inaccuracies will be crucial.

AI Overviews represent a significant leap forward in Google's quest to enhance the search experience through advanced artificial intelligence. While this innovation promises to deliver faster and more accurate answers to users, it also poses substantial challenges for web traffic and content creation. The reduced need for users to click through to external websites, combined with issues of content duplication and attribution, means that webmasters and content creators must adapt to a rapidly changing landscape.

The future of AI Overviews will likely involve greater personalization, deeper integration with other Google services, and heightened ethical and regulatory scrutiny. For those navigating this new frontier, staying informed about the latest developments and continuously refining content strategies will be essential for maintaining visibility and relevance in an AI-driven search environment.

Chapter 5: Winners and Losers: Traffic Redistribution

Platforms That Benefited

The digital ecosystem is a dynamic arena where changes in search engine algorithms can dramatically alter the fortunes of various online platforms. The recent updates to Google's algorithm, particularly the introduction of AI Overviews, have resulted in significant traffic redistribution, creating distinct winners and losers. Understanding which platforms benefited and why can offer valuable insights into the evolving landscape of digital content.

1. **Reddit**:
   - **Rise in Traffic:** Reddit emerged as one of the most significant beneficiaries of Google's algorithm updates. According to data from SEMrush, Reddit experienced a 126% growth in traffic from Google Search. This surge is attributed to Google's recognition of Reddit as a repository of authentic, user-generated content.
   - **Community Engagement**: Reddit's structure, based on user-generated content and community engagement, aligns well with Google's goal of surfacing content that provides real user experiences and insights. Users often append "Reddit" to their searches to find genuine

discussions and reviews, reinforcing the platform's authority.
- **Content Diversity:** The wide range of topics discussed on Reddit, from cooking and gardening to fashion and technology, ensures that it has relevant content for a vast array of search queries. This diversity makes Reddit a valuable resource for Google's AI models when generating comprehensive and contextually rich answers.

2. **Quora:**
- **Informative Content:** Quora, another user-generated content platform, saw significant gains as well. Quora's model of having experts and enthusiasts answer questions creates a rich repository of informative content. Google's AI Overviews frequently draw from Quora to provide detailed answers to user queries.
- **High-Quality Answers:** The platform's emphasis on quality answers and up voting useful responses aligns with Google's criteria for helpful content. This synergy has led to increased visibility and traffic for Quora, as Google's algorithms prioritize content that demonstrates expertise and reliability.

3. **Wikipedia:**
   - **Authority and Reliability:** Wikipedia has long been a trusted source of information due to its rigorous editorial standards and comprehensive coverage of topics. The recent updates have reinforced its prominence in search results, as Google seeks to ensure that users receive accurate and reliable information.
   - **Structured Data:** Wikipedia's structured and well-organized data format makes it an ideal candidate for Google's AI models to extract and present information. The platform's transparent citation practices and verifiable content further bolster its credibility.
4. **Instagram:**
   - **Visual Content:** Instagram's growth in traffic can be attributed to the increasing importance of visual content in search results. Google's algorithms have started to prioritize images and videos, recognizing that visual content can provide quick and engaging answers to user queries.
   - **Influencer Impact**: The platform's extensive use of influencers and user-generated content also plays a role. Influencers often create content that ranks highly due to its relevance and

engagement, driving more traffic from search results to Instagram.
5. **LinkedIn:**
   - **Professional Content:** LinkedIn has benefited from the shift towards more specialized and authoritative content. As Google's algorithms favor content that demonstrates expertise, LinkedIn's professional articles and posts are increasingly highlighted in search results.
   - **Industry Insights:** The platform's focus on industry insights, career advice, and professional development aligns well with Google's emphasis on high-quality, valuable content, leading to increased traffic and visibility.

Websites That Suffered

While some platforms have thrived under Google's new algorithm, many others have faced significant setbacks. Small and independent websites, in particular, have borne the brunt of these changes, with substantial reductions in traffic that threaten their viability.

1. **Small Independent Websites:**

- **Decreased Visibility:** Many small websites have seen their visibility in search results plummet. Despite often producing high-quality, niche content, these sites struggle to compete with larger, more established brands that now dominate the top search results.
- **Economic Impact:** The loss of traffic has direct economic consequences. Websites that rely on advertising revenue, affiliate links, or direct sales are finding it increasingly difficult to sustain their operations. For example, HouseFresh, a site dedicated to air purifier reviews, experienced a dramatic decline in traffic following the algorithm updates, leading to significant layoffs and financial strain.

2. **Niche Blogs and Specialist Sites:**
   - **Content Devaluation:** Specialist sites that offer in-depth knowledge on specific topics are often overshadowed by larger platforms that provide more general information. This devaluation of niche content means that users might miss out on detailed and expert insights.
   - **SEO Challenges:** The constant evolution of SEO best practices makes it challenging for small sites to keep up. Despite following Google's recommendations, many niche blogs and specialist sites find themselves losing ground to

competitors with more resources to invest in SEO.

3. **Content Farms and Low-Quality Sites:**
   - **Algorithm Penalties:** Websites known for producing low-quality, spammy content have been significantly affected by Google's updates. The algorithm changes are designed to demote such content, favoring more substantial and original information.
   - **Revenue Loss:** For these sites, the drop in search visibility translates directly into revenue loss. Many content farms, which rely on high volumes of traffic to generate ad revenue, are finding it increasingly difficult to maintain profitability.
4. **Media Outlets:**
   - **Reduced Organic Traffic:** Even well-established media outlets like New York Magazine and GQ have not been immune to the impacts of Google's updates. SEMrush data shows substantial reductions in their organic search traffic, affecting their overall reach and engagement.
   - **Content Adaptation:** Media outlets are now compelled to adapt their content strategies, focusing more on quality and engagement to

regain their search rankings. This shift often requires significant investments in editorial resources and SEO optimization.

5. **DIY and Hobbyist Sites:**
    - **Community Displacement:** Sites that cater to specific hobbies or DIY enthusiasts have seen traffic declines as platforms like Reddit gain prominence. These sites, which often rely on community contributions and detailed guides, are being overshadowed by more general user-generated content platforms.
    - **Monetization Challenges:** The drop in traffic impacts their ability to monetize through ads, sponsorships, and sales of related products or services. For instance, Ready Steady Cut, a UK-based entertainment news site, had to drastically reduce its team due to declining traffic and revenue.

The redistribution of traffic resulting from Google's algorithm updates highlights the complex and often unpredictable nature of digital content ecosystems. Platforms that align closely with Google's evolving criteria for quality and relevance, such as Reddit, Quora, Wikipedia, Instagram, and LinkedIn, have seen substantial gains. These platforms benefit from their ability to provide authentic, authoritative, and user-friendly content that meets Google's stringent standards.

On the other hand, many small and independent websites, niche blogs, content farms, media outlets, and DIY sites have faced significant challenges. Despite producing valuable and often highly specialized content, these sites struggle to maintain their visibility in an increasingly competitive search landscape. The economic impacts on these sites are profound, with many forced to downsize or rethink their business models entirely.

As the digital content landscape continues to evolve, webmasters and content creators must remain agile and adaptive. Understanding the factors that drive traffic distribution and leveraging strategies that align with Google's algorithmic priorities will be crucial for maintaining and growing their online presence. While the road ahead may be challenging, those who can navigate these changes effectively will find new opportunities to connect with audiences and achieve success in the ever-changing world of digital content.

Chapter 6

The Rise of User-Generated Content

Reddit, Quora, and Other Platforms

The recent updates to Google's search algorithm have sparked a significant shift in the landscape of web traffic, with user-generated content (UGC) platforms emerging as major beneficiaries. Among these platforms, Reddit and Quora stand out for their substantial growth in traffic and influence. This chapter delves into the reasons behind the rise of these UGC platforms, examining how they have capitalized on changes in search algorithms and user behavior to become essential destinations for information seekers.

Reddit

1. **Authenticity and Community Engagement:**

- **Authentic Discussions:** Reddit is renowned for its authentic and in-depth discussions. Unlike traditional websites that may prioritize polished, SEO-driven content, Reddit thrives on the genuine interactions between its users. These discussions often offer nuanced perspectives and firsthand experiences that resonate more with users.

- **Community Moderation:** Each subreddit is moderated by community members who enforce rules and maintain the quality of discussions. This self-regulation helps ensure that content remains relevant and valuable, fostering trust among users.

2. Diverse Content:

- **Wide Range of Topics:** Reddit hosts communities (subreddits) on virtually every topic imaginable, from highly technical subjects like programming and electronics to more niche interests like rare plants or vintage fashion. This diversity means that Reddit has relevant content for a wide array of search queries.

- **User Expertise:** Many subreddits are frequented by experts in their respective fields who provide high-quality, reliable information. For example, the "AskScience" subreddit features responses from qualified scientists, while "PersonalFinance" offers advice from financial professionals.

3. High Engagement:

- **Interactive Format**: The interactive nature of Reddit, where users can upvote, downvote, and comment on posts, creates a dynamic and engaging environment. This interaction not only improves the quality of content but also keeps users on the platform longer.

- **Real-Time Updates:** Reddit's format allows for real-time updates and discussions on breaking news and trending topics, making it a go-to source for timely information.

Quora

1. Expert Knowledge:

- **Qualified Respondents:** Quora attracts a wide range of experts, professionals, and enthusiasts who provide detailed answers to user questions. The platform's emphasis on credibility and expertise aligns well with Google's criteria for high-quality content.

- **Quality Over Quantity:** Unlike other platforms that may favor volume, Quora prioritizes the quality of responses. This focus on providing comprehensive, well-researched answers helps it rank highly in search results.

2. Structured Content:

- **Organized Format:** Quora's question-and-answer format is inherently structured, making it easy for search engines to index and retrieve relevant information. Each question page aggregates multiple answers, offering a variety of perspectives and insights.

- **SEO-Friendly:** Quora's content is naturally SEO-friendly due to its use of keywords in questions and answers. This structure ensures that Quora pages often appear in top search results for various queries.

3. Community Validation:

- **Upvotes and Downvotes:** Similar to Reddit, Quora uses a voting system to highlight the most helpful and accurate answers. This community validation mechanism ensures that the best content rises to the top, improving user trust and engagement.

- **Credibility Indicators:** Quora also allows users to include credentials and bios, adding another layer of credibility to the responses provided.

Other Platforms
1. Wikipedia:

- **Reliable Information:** Wikipedia remains a cornerstone of reliable information on the internet. Its strict editorial standards and extensive citation requirements ensure that the content is trustworthy and accurate.

- **Structured Data:** The well-organized structure of Wikipedia articles makes it easy for Google's algorithms to extract and present information, contributing to its high ranking in search results.

2. YouTube:

- **Visual Learning**: As a leading platform for video content, YouTube benefits from the increasing preference for visual learning. Tutorials, reviews, and educational videos often rank highly in search results, providing users with engaging and informative content.

- **Diverse Creators:** YouTube's vast array of content creators means there is a video for nearly every topic, from DIY projects to advanced academic lectures.

3. Instagram:

- Influencer Content: Instagram has seen a surge in traffic due to the popularity of influencer content. Influencers often create highly engaging and visually appealing posts that attract significant user interaction.

- **Visual Search:** The platform's focus on images and videos caters to users' growing preference for visual content, which is increasingly being prioritized by search algorithms.

Why These Sites Are Gaining Traffic

The rise of user-generated content platforms can be attributed to several key factors that align with both changing user behaviors and Google's evolving algorithmic priorities.

1. Authenticity and Trust:

- **Genuine Content**: Users are increasingly seeking out authentic, firsthand experiences and insights rather than polished, commercial content. UGC platforms excel in providing this type of genuine content, which resonates more with audiences.

- **Community Trust:** Platforms like Reddit and Quora build communities where users can trust the information due to the self-regulating nature of these communities. This trust translates into higher engagement and repeat visits.

2. Diversity and Depth of Content:

- **Comprehensive Coverage:** The vast array of topics covered by UGC platforms ensures that they have relevant content for almost any search query. This diversity is a significant advantage in capturing search traffic.

- **Detailed Responses:** UGC platforms often provide detailed and comprehensive responses to user queries, which align well with Google's goal of surfacing high-quality, in-depth content.

3. User Engagement:

- **Interactive Formats**: The interactive nature of platforms like Reddit and Quora, where users can vote on and comment on content, leads to higher engagement rates. This interaction signals to search engines that the content is valuable and relevant.

- **Timely Updates:** UGC platforms are often quicker to update content in response to new developments or trends, ensuring that the information remains current and relevant.

4. Alignment with Google's Algorithmic Changes:

- **Focus on Quality:** Google's algorithm updates have increasingly emphasized the importance of content quality, expertise, and user satisfaction. UGC platforms that prioritize these elements naturally align with Google's criteria for high-ranking content.

- **AI Integration**: Google's AI Overviews benefit from the structured and comprehensive nature of content on UGC platforms, which can be easily parsed and integrated into search results.

5. Shift in User Behavior:

- **Preference for Peer Reviews:** Users are increasingly looking for peer reviews and personal experiences, which are abundant on UGC platforms. This shift in user preference drives more traffic to these sites.

- **Search Trends:** Many users now add terms like "Reddit" or "Quora" to their search queries to find more personalized and trustworthy information. This behavior boosts the visibility and traffic of these platforms.

The rise of user-generated content platforms like Reddit, Quora, and others is a testament to the changing dynamics of web traffic and user preferences. As Google continues to refine its search algorithms to prioritize quality, authenticity, and user engagement, UGC platforms are well-positioned to capture a larger share of search traffic. Their ability to provide diverse, genuine, and comprehensive content that aligns with both user needs and search engine criteria has made them indispensable in the digital information ecosystem.

For website owners and content creators, understanding the factors driving the success of these platforms offers valuable lessons. Emphasizing authenticity, fostering community engagement, and ensuring the quality and relevance of content are crucial strategies for thriving in the current digital landscape. As user behaviors and search algorithms continue to evolve, staying attuned to these trends will be key to maintaining and growing an online presence.

Chapter 7

Case Study: House Fresh's Struggle

Building a Successful Niche Website

HouseFresh, a niche website dedicated to providing comprehensive air purifier reviews and indoor air quality information, emerged as a prime example of a successful independent publisher in the realm of digital content. Founded in 2020 by Gisele Navarro and her husband, HouseFresh quickly gained traction by offering in-depth, science-based reviews of air purifiers, backed by a decade of expertise in the field. Navarro's commitment to providing valuable, actionable information to consumers propelled HouseFresh into a thriving business, with a dedicated team of 15 employees and ambitious plans for the future.

1. Expertise and Authority:

- **Decade of Experience:** Navarro's extensive experience in writing about indoor air quality products positioned HouseFresh as a trusted authority in the niche. The website's content was characterized by rigorous testing methodologies, transparent review processes, and a commitment to providing unbiased recommendations.

- **Science-Based Approach:** HouseFresh distinguished itself by its scientific approach to product testing and evaluation. Navarro's background in environmental science lent credibility to the reviews, attracting users seeking reliable and evidence-based information.

2. User-Centric Focus:

- Addressing User Needs: HouseFresh's content was tailored to address the specific needs and concerns of consumers looking for air purifiers and related products. By providing answers to common questions, debunking myths, and offering practical advice, the website catered to the informational needs of its audience.

- **Transparency and Integrity:** Navarro's emphasis on transparency and integrity fostered trust among users. HouseFresh was upfront about its testing methodologies, potential biases, and affiliations, ensuring that users could make informed decisions based on reliable information.

3. Quality Content Creation:

- **Original and Engaging Content:** HouseFresh invested in creating original and engaging content that resonated with its target audience. From detailed product reviews to informative articles on indoor air quality, the website prioritized quality over quantity, aiming to provide value with every piece of content.

- **User-Friendly Interface:** HouseFresh's user-friendly interface and intuitive navigation made it easy for visitors to find relevant information quickly. The website's commitment to user experience contributed to high engagement and repeat visits.

The Impact of Google's Updates

Despite its initial success, HouseFresh found itself grappling with the far-reaching consequences of Google's algorithm updates, particularly the September 2023 and March 2024 updates, which significantly altered the dynamics of search engine rankings and traffic distribution.

1. Devastating Effects:

- **Dramatic Decline in Traffic:** The algorithm updates had a profound and immediate impact on

HouseFresh's visibility in search results. Keywords that once led users to HouseFresh were now directing them to larger lifestyle magazines and generic review sites, relegating HouseFresh to obscurity.

- **Loss of Revenue and Viability:** The drastic decline in traffic dealt a severe blow to HouseFresh's revenue and long-term viability. With fewer visitors accessing the website, advertising revenue dwindled, and the prospect of sustaining a team of 15 employees became increasingly untenable.

2. Survival Strategies:

- **Adaptation Efforts:** In response to the algorithm updates, HouseFresh implemented various adaptation strategies in a bid to salvage its online presence. These efforts included revising content to align with Google's evolving criteria, optimizing keywords, and exploring alternative traffic sources.

- **Consultation and Expertise:** Navarro sought consultation from SEO experts and industry professionals to navigate the complexities of the algorithmic changes. Despite her efforts to comply with Google's guidelines and recommendations, the impact on HouseFresh's traffic and revenue remained significant.

3. Reflections and Resilience:

- **Navigating Uncertainty:** The challenges posed by Google's algorithm updates forced Navarro to reflect on the volatile nature of the digital landscape and the inherent risks of relying solely on search engine traffic. The experience underscored the importance of diversifying traffic sources and building resilience against algorithmic fluctuations.

- **Commitment to Quality:** Throughout the ordeal, Navarro remained steadfast in her commitment to delivering quality content and serving her audience. Despite the setbacks, HouseFresh continued to uphold its standards of excellence, albeit against formidable odds.

The case of HouseFresh serves as a poignant reminder of the precariousness of success in the digital realm and the profound impact that algorithmic changes can have on even the most meticulously curated websites. Despite HouseFresh's commendable efforts to provide valuable content and adhere to best practices, it ultimately fell victim to the unpredictable shifts in search engine rankings and traffic distribution.

As website owners and content creators grapple with the aftermath of Google's updates, the case of HouseFresh offers valuable insights into the importance of resilience, adaptation, and diversification. Niche websites like HouseFresh must remain vigilant in monitoring algorithmic changes, exploring alternative traffic sources, and prioritizing user-centricity to mitigate the risks of reliance on search engine traffic alone. While the road ahead may be fraught with challenges, the determination and resilience demonstrated by Navarro and her team underscore the enduring value of quality content and unwavering commitment to serving the needs of the audience.

Chapter 8

Adapting to Change: Strategies for Survival

SEO Best Practices Post-Update

The seismic shifts in Google's search algorithm have compelled website owners and content creators to reassess their SEO strategies and adapt to the evolving digital landscape. In this chapter, we explore the key SEO best practices post-update and examine how website owners can navigate the complexities of algorithmic changes to maintain visibility and relevance in search results.

1. Quality Over Quantity:

- **Focus on User Intent:** Rather than prioritizing keyword density or volume of content, focus on understanding and fulfilling user intent. Craft content that directly addresses the needs and queries of your target audience, providing valuable and actionable insights.

- **Comprehensive Content:** Aim to create comprehensive, authoritative content that covers topics in-depth and offers unique perspectives or insights. Google's emphasis on expertise, authority, and trustworthiness (E-A-T) means that high-quality, comprehensive content is more likely to rank well.

2. Semantic Search Optimization:

- **Natural Language Processing:** With the rise of AI-driven search algorithms, including BERT (Bidirectional Encoder Representations from Transformers), optimizing for semantic search has become increasingly important. Structure your content to reflect natural language patterns and semantic relationships between words and phrases.

- **Contextual Relevance:** Google's algorithms now prioritize contextually relevant content that comprehensively addresses the topic at hand. Incorporate relevant keywords and synonyms naturally throughout your content to signal to search engines the depth and relevance of your content.

3. User Experience Optimization:

- **Mobile-Friendly Design:** Given the prevalence of mobile browsing, ensure that your website is optimized for mobile devices. Responsive design, fast loading times, and intuitive navigation are essential for providing a seamless user experience across all devices.

- **Engagement Metrics:** Google considers user engagement metrics, such as click-through rate (CTR), bounce rate, and dwell time, as indicators of content quality and relevance. Encourage user interaction and engagement by creating compelling, visually appealing content and intuitive navigation pathways.

4. Technical SEO Optimization:

- **Site Speed and Performance:** Page speed and overall site performance are crucial ranking factors. Optimize your website's loading times, minimize server response times, and leverage caching and compression techniques to enhance user experience and improve search engine rankings.

- **Structured Data Markup:** Implement structured data markup, such as schema.org, to provide search engines with additional context and metadata about your content. Structured data can enhance rich snippets, improve click-through rates, and increase visibility in search results.

Alternative Traffic Sources

In light of the volatility and unpredictability of search engine traffic, diversifying traffic sources is imperative for safeguarding against sudden drops in visibility and revenue. Here are several alternative traffic sources that website owners can leverage to mitigate reliance on search engine traffic alone:

1. Social Media Marketing:

- Engagement and Outreach: Utilize social media platforms, such as Facebook, Twitter, Instagram, and LinkedIn, to engage with your audience, promote your content, and foster community engagement. Build a strong social media presence by sharing valuable content, responding to comments and messages, and participating in relevant discussions.

- Paid Advertising: Explore paid advertising options on social media platforms to target specific demographics, amplify your reach, and drive traffic to your website. Experiment with different ad formats, targeting parameters, and messaging to optimize your advertising campaigns for maximum effectiveness.

2. Email Marketing:

- List Building and Segmentation: Build an email subscriber list and segment your subscribers based on their interests, preferences, and behaviors. Create personalized email campaigns that deliver relevant content, promotions, and updates to each segment, fostering engagement and driving traffic to your website.

- Automation and Drip Campaigns: Implement email automation and drip campaigns to nurture leads, onboard new subscribers, and re-engage inactive users. Use automated workflows to deliver targeted content at each stage of the customer journey, from awareness to conversion.

3. Content Syndication and Guest Posting:

- Syndication Platforms: Syndicate your content on reputable platforms and networks to reach new audiences and amplify your content's visibility. Submit guest posts to industry publications, blogs, and forums to establish thought leadership, build backlinks, and drive referral traffic to your website.

- Cross-Promotion: Collaborate with other content creators, influencers, and brands to cross-promote each other's content and reach mutually beneficial audiences. Participate in content swaps, joint webinars, and collaborative projects to expand your reach and diversify your audience base.

4. Community Engagement and Forums:

- **Online Communities:** Participate in online forums, discussion groups, and community websites relevant to your niche or industry. Engage in conversations, answer questions, and share valuable insights to establish credibility, build relationships, and drive traffic back to your website.

- **Q&A Platforms:** Join question-and-answer platforms, such as Quora and Stack Exchange, to provide expert answers to user queries and showcase your expertise. Include links to relevant content on your website to drive traffic and encourage further engagement.

In an era marked by rapid technological advancements and algorithmic upheavals, the ability to adapt and innovate is paramount for website owners and content creators. By embracing SEO best practices tailored to the post-update landscape and diversifying traffic sources beyond search engines, businesses can fortify their online presence, enhance resilience, and thrive amidst uncertainty. While the challenges of navigating algorithmic changes and evolving consumer behaviors may be daunting, the opportunities for growth and innovation are equally abundant for those willing to embrace change and chart new paths to success.

Chapter 9

The Role of Content Quality

What Google Considers "Helpful Content"

In an era where information overload is ubiquitous, Google's mission to organize the world's information and make it universally accessible and useful has never been more pertinent. Central to Google's algorithmic updates is the concept of "helpful content" – content that not only satisfies user queries but also provides valuable, trustworthy, and authoritative information. In this chapter, we delve into what Google considers "helpful content" and explore the key factors that contribute to content quality in the eyes of search engines.

1. Relevance and Context:

- **Understanding User Intent:** Google prioritizes content that aligns with user intent and contextually addresses the specific needs and queries of searchers. Content creators must thoroughly research and analyze user intent for target keywords to ensure that their content resonates with the audience and fulfills their informational needs.

- **Comprehensive Coverage**: Helpful content provides comprehensive coverage of the topic at hand, addressing key aspects, answering common questions, and offering actionable insights. By providing in-depth information and addressing potential follow-up queries, content creators can enhance the relevance and usefulness of their content.

2. Expertise, Authoritativeness, and Trustworthiness (E-A-T):

- **Demonstrating Expertise:** Google places a premium on content created by subject matter experts who demonstrate expertise, authority, and trustworthiness (E-A-T) in their respective fields. Content creators should showcase their credentials, qualifications, and industry expertise to establish credibility and trust with both users and search engines.

- **Credible Sources and Citations:** Helpful content cites authoritative sources, references, and citations to substantiate claims, validate information, and enhance credibility. By leveraging reputable sources and citing credible references, content creators can reinforce the trustworthiness of their content and position themselves as reliable sources of information.

3. Readability and Accessibility:

- **Clear and Concise Writing:** Google values content that is written in a clear, concise, and easily understandable manner, catering to users of varying literacy levels and backgrounds. Content creators should prioritize readability by using simple language, avoiding jargon, and breaking down complex concepts into digestible chunks.

- **Structured Formatting:** Helpful content employs structured formatting, such as headings, subheadings, bullet points, and numbered lists, to improve readability and facilitate skimming and scanning. By organizing content into logical sections and using visual cues to guide readers, content creators can enhance user experience and engagement.

Creating Content That Ranks

While understanding Google's criteria for helpful content is crucial, content creators must also possess the requisite skills and strategies to create content that ranks prominently in search engine results pages

(SERPs). Here are some key considerations for creating content that ranks:

1. Keyword Research and Optimization:

- **Identify Target Keywords:** Conduct thorough keyword research to identify relevant, high-intent keywords that align with your content's topic and audience. Use keyword research tools to analyze search volume, competition, and user intent to inform your content strategy.

- **Strategic Placement:** Incorporate target keywords strategically throughout your content, including in titles, headings, meta tags, and body text. Optimize on-page elements, such as URL structure and image alt attributes, to signal to search engines the relevance and focus of your content.

2. Content Depth and Breadth:

- **Comprehensive Coverage**: Create content that offers comprehensive coverage of the topic, addressing key subtopics, related questions, and potential user queries. Aim to provide depth and breadth in your content, exploring different angles, perspectives, and insights to enrich the user experience.

- **Long-Form Content:** Long-form content tends to perform well in search results, as it allows content creators to delve into complex topics, provide detailed explanations, and offer valuable insights. While length alone does not guarantee quality, long-form content often outperforms shorter counterparts in terms of user engagement and search visibility.

3. Engaging Multimedia Elements:

- **Visual Enhancements:** Incorporate engaging multimedia elements, such as images, videos, infographics, and interactive elements, to enhance the visual appeal and interactivity of your content. Visuals not only break up the text and improve readability but also cater to different learning preferences and enhance user engagement.

- **Optimized Media:** Optimize multimedia elements for search by using descriptive filenames, alt tags, and captions that include relevant keywords. Ensure that multimedia assets are properly formatted, compressed for web use, and accessible to all users, including those with disabilities.

In the ever-evolving landscape of search engine optimization (SEO), content quality remains paramount for achieving sustained visibility, relevance, and credibility in search engine results. By understanding Google's criteria for helpful content and adhering to best practices for content creation, content creators can position themselves for success in the competitive digital ecosystem. Whether through relevance, expertise, readability, or multimedia engagement, the pursuit of content excellence is both an art and a science—one that requires continuous refinement, adaptation, and innovation in response to changing algorithms, user behaviors, and industry trends.

Chapter 10

Google's War on Spam

Identifying Low-Quality Content

In its quest to provide users with the most relevant and reliable information, Google has waged a relentless war on spammy and low-quality content. The proliferation of spammy practices not only degrades the user experience but also undermines the integrity of search results. In this chapter, we delve into how Google identifies low-quality content and the measures it employs to combat spammy practices effectively.

1. Content Relevance and Originality:

- **Duplicate Content Detection:** Google employs sophisticated algorithms to detect and penalize duplicate content, which refers to content that appears verbatim or nearly identical across multiple web pages. Duplicate content diminishes the user experience and dilutes the authority of original sources.

- **Thin Content Detection:** Google scrutinizes the quality and depth of content, penalizing websites that publish thin, shallow, or insubstantial content devoid of substantive value. Content that lacks depth, originality, or relevance to user queries is deemed low-quality and may incur penalties in search rankings.

2. User Experience Signals:

- **High Bounce Rates:** Websites with high bounce rates, indicative of users quickly navigating away from a page without engaging further, may signal low-quality or irrelevant content. Google interprets high bounce rates as a negative user signal, potentially resulting in lower search rankings.

- **Low Dwell Time:** Dwell time, the duration users spend actively engaging with a webpage before returning to search results, is another user experience signal evaluated by Google. Low dwell times may suggest that users did not find the content valuable or relevant to their needs.

3. Link Quality and Authority:

- **Backlink Profile Analysis:** Google assesses the quality, relevance, and authority of backlinks pointing to a website to determine its credibility and trustworthiness. Websites with a diverse, natural, and authoritative backlink profile are more likely to rank higher in search results.

- Link Farm Detection: Google combats manipulative link-building tactics, such as link farms and link schemes, which artificially inflate a website's backlink profile through spammy or irrelevant links. Websites engaged in such practices risk penalties and loss of search visibility.

Measures to Combat Spammy Practices

To maintain the integrity and reliability of its search results, Google employs a multifaceted approach to combat spammy practices and ensure the delivery of high-quality content to users. Here are some key measures taken by Google to combat spam:

1. Algorithmic Updates:

- **Continuous Refinement:** Google regularly updates its search algorithms to refine its ability to detect and penalize spammy practices effectively. Algorithmic updates, such as Panda, Penguin, and BERT, target specific types of spam and improve the overall quality of search results.

- **Machine Learning and AI:** Google leverages machine learning and artificial intelligence (AI) technologies to enhance its spam detection capabilities and adapt to emerging spam tactics. By analyzing vast amounts of data and patterns, machine learning models can identify and penalize spam at scale.

2. Manual Actions:

- Manual Review Process: In addition to automated algorithms, Google employs a team of human reviewers to manually assess and address instances of spammy or low-quality content. Manual actions, such as manual penalties or demotions, are applied to websites that violate Google's quality guidelines.

- **Reconsideration Requests:** Website owners can submit reconsideration requests to Google after addressing issues identified by manual actions. Google reviews these requests and may lift penalties if the website demonstrates compliance with quality guidelines.

3. Quality Guidelines and Webmaster Resources:

- Transparent Guidelines: Google provides clear and transparent quality guidelines for webmasters, outlining best practices for creating high-quality, user-centric content. By adhering to these guidelines, website owners can align their content with Google's expectations and avoid penalties.

- **Educational Resources:** Google offers a range of educational resources, including webmaster forums, blog posts, and help documentation, to help website owners understand and comply with its quality guidelines. These resources empower webmasters to improve their websites' quality and performance in search results.

Google's relentless pursuit of high-quality search results underscores its commitment to delivering a valuable and trustworthy user experience. By identifying and combatting spammy practices through a combination of algorithmic updates, manual actions, and quality guidelines, Google strives to elevate the quality of content available on the web and safeguard the integrity of its search ecosystem. While the battle against spam remains ongoing, Google's proactive measures and continuous innovation signal its dedication to maintaining a fair, relevant, and user-centric search experience for millions of users worldwide.

Chapter 11

AI and Search Accuracy

Strengths and Weaknesses of AI Overviews

As Google embraces AI-powered search features, including AI Overviews, it heralds a new era of search accuracy and efficiency. However, with innovation comes challenges and complexities. In this chapter, we explore the strengths and weaknesses of AI Overviews and their impact on search accuracy.

1. Strengths of AI Overviews:

- **Speed and Efficiency:** AI Overviews leverage machine learning algorithms to quickly generate concise summaries of search queries, providing users with immediate answers to their questions. This speed and efficiency enhance user experience and streamline information retrieval.

- **Comprehensive Coverage:** AI Overviews draw from a diverse range of sources to provide users with comprehensive insights into various topics. By aggregating information from multiple sources, AI

Overviews offer a holistic perspective on search queries, enriching user understanding.

- **Accessibility and Convenience:** AI Overviews make information more accessible and digestible for users, particularly those on mobile devices or with limited time. By condensing complex information into bite-sized summaries, AI Overviews cater to users' preferences for quick, easy-to-digest content.

2. Weaknesses of AI Overviews:

- **Lack of Contextual Understanding:** Despite advancements in natural language processing, AI Overviews may struggle to grasp the nuances and context of search queries, leading to inaccuracies or oversimplifications. Contextual understanding is crucial for providing relevant and accurate information.

- **Limited Depth and Detail:** AI Overviews prioritize brevity and conciseness, which may result in oversimplification or omission of important details. Users seeking in-depth insights or nuanced perspectives may find AI Overviews lacking in depth and detail, limiting their utility for certain queries.

- **Potential for Misinterpretation:** AI Overviews rely on algorithms to interpret and summarize information, which may lead to misinterpretations or errors, particularly with complex or ambiguous queries. Users must exercise caution and critical thinking when relying on AI-generated summaries.

Real-World Examples of AI Missteps

While AI Overviews hold promise for enhancing search accuracy, real-world examples highlight instances where AI missteps have occurred, underscoring the importance of ongoing refinement and improvement.

1. Misleading Summaries:

- **Misrepresentation of Facts:** In some cases, AI Overviews may inadvertently misrepresent facts or present misleading information due to algorithmic limitations or biases. Users may encounter inaccuracies or distortions in AI-generated summaries, leading to confusion or misinformation.

- **Ambiguous Interpretations:** AI Overviews may struggle to disambiguate ambiguous queries or infer context accurately, resulting in misleading interpretations or incomplete summaries. Ambiguities in language or semantics pose challenges for AI algorithms, leading to errors or inaccuracies.

2. Lack of Nuance:

- **Oversimplification:** AI Overviews may oversimplify complex topics or issues, glossing over nuances or subtleties that require deeper understanding. Users seeking nuanced insights or detailed analysis may find AI-generated summaries inadequate or superficial, limiting their usefulness.

- **Bias and Subjectivity:** AI algorithms may inadvertently introduce bias or subjectivity into summaries, reflecting inherent biases in training data or algorithmic decision-making processes. Biased or skewed summaries may perpetuate stereotypes or misconceptions, undermining the integrity of search results.

AI Overviews represent a significant advancement in search technology, offering users faster access to information and streamlined search experiences. However, their strengths must be balanced against their weaknesses and limitations, including potential inaccuracies, lack of depth, and susceptibility to biases. As AI continues to evolve and mature, addressing these challenges will be crucial for enhancing search accuracy and ensuring that AI Overviews deliver reliable, relevant, and trustworthy information to users worldwide. By fostering transparency, accountability, and ongoing refinement, Google can harness the power of AI to empower users with knowledge and insights while mitigating the risks of misinformation and bias.

Chapter 12

The Business Side: Financial Implications

Revenue Impact on Small vs. Large Websites

As Google's algorithm updates reshape the digital landscape, the financial implications for website owners, both large and small, are profound. In this chapter, we examine the revenue impact on small and large websites and the long-term economic consequences of these changes.

1. Small Websites:

- **Vulnerability to Algorithm Changes:** Small websites, often operated by individuals or small teams, are particularly vulnerable to the fluctuations caused by Google's algorithm updates. A sudden drop in search rankings can have devastating financial repercussions, as these websites rely heavily on organic traffic for revenue generation.

- **Dependency on Google Traffic:** Small websites may have limited resources to diversify their traffic sources, making them overly reliant on Google for traffic acquisition. When algorithm changes result in decreased visibility or traffic loss, small website owners may struggle to sustain their businesses and generate revenue.
- **Revenue Loss and Financial Strain:** A significant decrease in Google traffic can lead to a sharp decline in ad revenue, affiliate earnings, and other monetization channels for small websites. This loss of income can create financial strain and jeopardize the viability of the business, forcing website owners to reassess their strategies and priorities.

2. Large Websites:

- **Resilience to Algorithm Updates:** Large websites with established brands and diversified revenue streams are generally more resilient to the impact of algorithm updates. While fluctuations in search rankings may still occur, these websites have the resources and expertise to adapt their strategies and mitigate potential revenue losses.

- **Diversification of Revenue Streams:** Large websites often have multiple revenue streams, including advertising, subscription services, e-commerce, and sponsored content. Diversifying revenue sources reduces dependence on Google traffic and minimizes the financial impact of algorithm changes.
- **Strategic Adaptation:** Large websites can leverage their scale and resources to strategically adapt to algorithm updates and changes in user behavior. By investing in content quality, user experience enhancements, and innovative monetization strategies, large website owners can maintain their competitive edge and sustain revenue growth.

Long-Term Economic Consequences

The long-term economic consequences of Google's algorithm updates extend beyond immediate revenue fluctuations, shaping the broader landscape of online commerce and digital entrepreneurship.

1. **Market Consolidation:**

- **Dominance of Established Players:** Algorithm updates that favor large, authoritative websites may exacerbate market consolidation, further entrenching the dominance of established players. Small and independent websites may struggle to compete against industry giants, leading to a less diverse and competitive online ecosystem.
- **Barriers to Entry:** The increasing complexity of SEO and the dominance of large websites create significant barriers to entry for new entrants and aspiring entrepreneurs. The high costs of competing for visibility and traffic on Google's search results page may deter innovation and limit opportunities for small businesses to thrive.

2. **Innovation and Creativity:**

- **Incentives for Quality Content:** Google's emphasis on content quality and user satisfaction incentivizes website owners to prioritize valuable, informative, and engaging content. As competition intensifies, content creators must innovate and

differentiate themselves to stand out in crowded markets, fostering creativity and innovation.
- **Emergence of Niche Markets:** Algorithm updates that prioritize relevance and expertise may lead to the emergence of niche markets and specialized content ecosystems. Smaller websites that excel in niche areas can carve out a competitive advantage and attract dedicated audiences, driving innovation and diversity in content offerings.

Google's algorithm updates exert a profound influence on the financial dynamics of the online ecosystem, shaping the revenue landscape for website owners of all sizes. While small websites face heightened vulnerability and financial strain in the face of algorithmic fluctuations, large websites possess greater resilience and adaptability to navigate market challenges. The long-term economic consequences of these updates extend beyond revenue fluctuations, impacting market competition, innovation, and entrepreneurship in the digital age. By understanding and anticipating the financial implications of Google's algorithm updates, website owners can proactively adapt their strategies, diversify their revenue streams, and foster resilience in an ever-evolving digital landscape.

Chapter 13

Legal and Ethical Considerations

Antitrust Lawsuits Against Google

Google's dominant position in the search engine market has drawn scrutiny from regulators around the world, leading to a series of antitrust lawsuits aimed at addressing concerns about its market power and competitive practices.

1. Allegations of Monopoly Power:

- **Market Dominance:** Google controls over 90% of the global search engine market, giving it unprecedented market power and influence over online commerce and information dissemination. Regulators allege that Google's dominance stifles competition and innovation, limiting consumer choice and harming rival businesses.
- **Anticompetitive Practices**: Antitrust lawsuits accuse Google of engaging in anticompetitive practices, including preferential treatment of its own services in search results, exclusionary

contracts with device manufacturers, and anti-competitive acquisitions that eliminate potential rivals.

2. Legal Challenges:

- **US Department of Justice Lawsuit:** In October 2020, the US Department of Justice filed a landmark antitrust lawsuit against Google, accusing the tech giant of unlawfully maintaining monopolies in search and search advertising. The lawsuit seeks to break up Google's alleged monopoly power and restore competition in the digital marketplace.
- **State Attorneys General Lawsuits:** A coalition of state attorney's general has filed separate antitrust lawsuits against Google, alleging similar violations of antitrust laws and seeking remedies to address the company's anti-competitive conduct. These lawsuits aim to hold Google accountable for its alleged abuse of market power and promote fair competition in the digital economy.

Ethical Concerns in Algorithm Changes

Google's algorithm updates play a pivotal role in shaping the online ecosystem, influencing the visibility and accessibility of information for billions of users worldwide. However, these algorithm changes raise ethical concerns related to transparency, fairness, and accountability.

1. Transparency and Disclosure:

- **Opaque Decision-Making:** Google's algorithms operate behind a veil of secrecy, with limited transparency into the factors and criteria used to rank search results. This lack of transparency raises concerns about accountability and fairness, as website owners and users have little visibility into the rationale behind search rankings and algorithmic decisions.
- **Need for Disclosure:** Ethical considerations dictate the importance of transparency and disclosure in algorithmic processes, enabling stakeholders to understand how decisions are made and assess the potential biases or impacts of algorithmic changes. Greater transparency can

enhance trust and accountability in Google's search ecosystem.

2. Fairness and Bias:

- **Algorithmic Bias:** Google's algorithms may inadvertently perpetuate biases and inequalities in search results, reflecting underlying societal biases or systemic inequalities. Biased algorithms can reinforce stereotypes, marginalize underrepresented voices, and amplify misinformation, undermining the integrity and fairness of search results.
- **Mitigating Bias:** Ethical considerations urge Google to mitigate bias in its algorithms through rigorous testing, diversity in data sources, and proactive measures to identify and address algorithmic biases. By promoting fairness and inclusivity in search results, Google can uphold ethical principles and foster a more equitable online environment.

The legal and ethical considerations surrounding Google's algorithm updates underscore the complex interplay between market dynamics, regulatory scrutiny, and ethical responsibilities in the digital age. Antitrust lawsuits against Google highlight concerns about market concentration and anti-competitive behavior, while ethical concerns focus on transparency, fairness, and accountability in algorithmic processes. As Google navigates these legal and ethical challenges, it must balance its business interests with its obligations to promote competition, protect user privacy, and uphold ethical principles in algorithmic decision-making. By addressing these considerations thoughtfully and transparently, Google can foster trust, accountability, and integrity in its search ecosystem, contributing to a more open, fair, and equitable digital landscape.

Chapter 14

The Future of Search

Predictions for Upcoming Google Updates

As Google continues to innovate and refine its search algorithms, speculation abounds regarding the direction of future updates and their potential impact on the digital landscape. In this chapter, we explore predictions for upcoming Google updates and their implications for website owners, marketers, and users.

1. Emphasis on User Experience:

- **Core Web Vitals**: Google's recent focus on Core Web Vitals, which measure aspects of user experience such as page loading speed, interactivity, and visual stability, suggests that future updates may prioritize user-centric metrics. Websites that prioritize user experience and optimize for Core Web Vitals are likely to see improved search rankings and visibility.

- **Mobile-First Indexing:** With the prevalence of mobile devices, Google may place greater emphasis on mobile-first indexing, prioritizing mobile-friendly websites in search results. Website owners should prioritize mobile optimization to ensure compatibility and accessibility across devices.

2. Enhanced AI Integration:

- **Advancements in Natural Language Processing:** Google's investment in natural language processing (NLP) technologies indicates a shift towards more sophisticated AI-driven search experiences. Future updates may leverage NLP to better understand user intent, context, and semantics, delivering more relevant and personalized search results.
- **Expansion of AI Overviews**: AI-generated summaries, or AI Overviews, are likely to become more prevalent in search results, providing users with concise answers and insights extracted from multiple sources. Website owners should optimize their content for AI Overviews by providing clear,

structured information that aligns with user queries.

3. Focus on E-A-T and Expertise:

- **E-A-T (Expertise, Authoritativeness, Trustworthiness):** Google's emphasis on E-A-T signals a continued focus on content quality and credibility. Websites that demonstrate expertise, authority, and trustworthiness in their respective fields are likely to receive preferential treatment in search rankings. Investing in authoritative content and building trust with users are key strategies for future success.
- **Expertise Recognition:** Google may increasingly rely on signals of expertise, such as author credentials, industry recognition, and user feedback, to evaluate the quality and relevance of content. Website owners should prioritize showcasing their expertise and credentials to enhance their visibility and credibility in search results.

Preparing for an AI-Driven Search Landscape

As Google continues to integrate AI technologies into its search algorithms, website owners and marketers must adapt to an increasingly AI-driven search landscape. Here are some strategies for preparing for the future of search:

1. Content Optimization:

- **Structured Data Markup:** Implement structured data markup to provide context and metadata that helps search engines understand the content of your website. Structured data enhances visibility in search results and facilitates the generation of AI Overviews.
- **Semantic SEO:** Focus on semantic SEO strategies that align with Google's evolving understanding of natural language and user intent. Create content that answers specific questions, addresses user needs, and provides value-added insights.

2. User Engagement and Retention:

- **Interactive Content:** Create interactive and engaging content experiences that encourage user interaction and participation. Features such as quizzes, polls, and interactive tools can enhance user engagement and prolong time on site, signaling quality and relevance to search engines.
- **Personalization:** Leverage personalization techniques to tailor content and recommendations to individual user preferences and interests. By delivering personalized experiences, you can enhance user satisfaction and retention, driving repeat visits and engagement.

3. Adaptability and Innovation:

- **Agility in Optimization:** Stay informed about industry trends, algorithm updates, and best practices for search optimization. Maintain agility and flexibility in your optimization strategies to adapt to changing search algorithms and user behaviors.
- **Experimentation and Innovation:** Embrace experimentation and innovation in content creation, user experience design, and optimization techniques. Test new ideas, iterate

on successful strategies, and continuously evolve your approach to stay ahead of the curve.

The future of search promises continued evolution and innovation, driven by advancements in AI technology, user-centric design principles, and changing user behaviors. By anticipating upcoming Google updates and preparing for an AI-driven search landscape, website owners and marketers can position themselves for success in an increasingly competitive and dynamic digital environment. By prioritizing user experience, content quality, and adaptability, businesses can thrive amidst the shifting sands of search optimization, delivering value to users and staying ahead of the curve in the ever-evolving world of search.

Conclusion

In this book, we have delved into the intricacies of Google's algorithm updates and their profound implications for the digital landscape. From the evolution of search to the rise of AI-driven technologies, we have explored the far-reaching impacts of these changes on website owners, marketers, and users alike. As we conclude our exploration, let us recap the key insights and offer final thoughts on navigating the new search environment.

Recap of Key Insights

1. **Evolution of Google Search:** We traced the evolution of Google Search from its humble beginnings to its current status as the dominant player in the search engine market. Over the years, Google has continually refined its algorithms to deliver more relevant and personalized search results to users.
2. **Impact of Algorithm Updates:** We examined the significant impact of Google's algorithm

updates on website rankings, traffic patterns, and revenue streams. Updates such as the September 2023 and March 2024 changes have reshaped the search landscape, causing upheaval for many website owners and marketers.

3. **Rise of AI Overviews:** Google's introduction of AI Overviews represents a paradigm shift in search technology, with AI-generated summaries providing users with quick answers to their queries. While these AI-driven features offer convenience, they also raise concerns about content attribution and accuracy.

4. **Traffic Redistribution:** The emergence of user-generated content platforms like Reddit, Quora, and Instagram has altered traffic patterns on the web, with some websites experiencing significant traffic declines while others thrive. Understanding these shifts is essential for website owners seeking to adapt to the changing search environment.

5. **Legal and Ethical Considerations**: Antitrust lawsuits against Google and ethical concerns surrounding algorithmic transparency and bias highlight the complex legal and ethical considerations inherent in the search ecosystem. Balancing innovation with accountability is crucial for fostering trust and integrity in search.

6. **Future of Search:** Looking ahead, we anticipate further advancements in AI-driven technologies, increased emphasis on user experience and content quality, and ongoing challenges in navigating regulatory landscapes and ethical dilemmas. Preparing for the future of search requires adaptability, innovation, and a commitment to user-centric principles.

Final Thoughts on Navigating the New Search Environment

As website owners, marketers, and users navigate the ever-changing landscape of search, several guiding principles can help steer us towards success:

1. **Prioritize User Experience:** Focus on creating high-quality, user-centric content that meets the needs and preferences of your target audience. Invest in optimizing website performance, mobile responsiveness, and overall usability to enhance user satisfaction and engagement.
2. **Stay Informed and Agile:** Keep abreast of industry trends, algorithm updates, and best practices for search optimization. Maintain

agility and flexibility in your strategies to adapt to changing search algorithms and user behaviors.
3. **Embrace Innovation:** Embrace experimentation and innovation in content creation, optimization techniques, and user engagement strategies. Explore new avenues for reaching and connecting with your audience, and don't be afraid to think outside the box.
4. **Uphold Ethical Standards:** Prioritize transparency, fairness, and accountability in your practices, adhering to ethical standards and regulatory guidelines. Build trust with your audience by demonstrating integrity, authenticity, and respect for user privacy.
5. **Collaborate and Learn:** Foster collaboration and knowledge-sharing within the industry, learning from peers, experts, and thought leaders. By staying connected and sharing insights, we can collectively navigate the complexities of the new search environment and drive positive change.

In conclusion, the future of search holds both challenges and opportunities for website owners, marketers, and users. By embracing innovation, prioritizing user experience, and upholding ethical standards, we can navigate these challenges and harness the power of search to create value, foster engagement, and enrich the digital experience for all. Together, let us embark on this journey towards a more informed, connected, and accessible online world.

www.ingramcontent.com/pod-product-compliance
Lightning Source LLC
Chambersburg PA
CBHW050108230526
45470CB00004B/1738